FAITH VIBES

VOLUME 1

Deepening Your Prayer Life

"DAILY BOOSTS FOR A STRONGER SPIRIT"

FAITHVIBES

Deepening Your Prayer Life

Faith Vibes 21 Day Devotional
Volume 1: Deepening Your Prayer Life
© 2024 Celeste Payne

Publisher:
Celeste Empowers
staff@celesteempowers.com
celesteempowers.com/contact
(855) 213-4345
ISBN: 978-1-930276-99-4

This book is a work of nonfiction. The author has made every effort to ensure the accuracy of the information herein. However, the information contained in this book is provided without warranty, either express or implied.

First Edition: October 2024

FAITHVIBES
Deepening Your Prayer Life

Introduction

Let us then approach God's throne of grace with confidence, so that we may receive mercy and find grace to help us in our time of need.

MATTHEW 6:6

Welcome to "Faith Vibes: Volume 1 - Deepening Your Prayer Life," a transformative 21-day journey designed to enrich your spiritual connection and elevate your prayer practice. In the midst of life's demands, carving out moments for reflection can be a challenge. This volume serves as your personal retreat, guiding you to explore the profound impact of prayer through daily reflections, scripture, and journaling prompts.

Throughout these pages, you will uncover insights into God's promises and how they manifest in your life. From finding peace and strength to embracing healing and guidance, "Faith Vibes" invites you to experience prayer as a source of comfort and empowerment. Whether you're seeking to deepen your spiritual practice or explore new facets of faith, this book offers a path to a more meaningful and prayerful life.

Begin this journey with an open heart and witness the growth of your faith, one prayer at a time.

FAITHVIBES

Deepening Your Prayer Life

Celeste Payne is a dynamic entrepreneur and creative visionary, passionately leading two organizations: Celeste Empowers and Arts Empowered. With a focus on empowering women through art classes and coaching, Celeste provides a wide range of services, including Canva support, book writing, publishing, and product design. Her commitment to community engagement shines through Arts Empowered, where she hosts vibrant paint parties for children, fostering creativity and joy. Celeste is also an author, with works like "The Amazing Spelling Dictionary," "Faith Vibes," "I Love Me Some Me," and God Has A Miracle for You" capturing her inspirational spirit. As an ordained minister, Celeste is on a mission is to lead globally in business and ministry, blending her passion for art and faith to uplift and inspire others.

Connect with the Faith Vibes Movement at empowermentsessions.com

facebook.com/celesteempowersnow

@empowerment4u

FAITHVIBES

Deepening Your Prayer Life

10 Ways God Responds to Prayer

"But when you pray, go into your room,
close the door and pray to your Father,
who is unseen."

MATTHEW 6:6

1   **God Listens to Our Prayers**
"The Lord is near to all who call on him, to all who call on him in truth." - Psalm 145:18

2   **God Grants Wisdom**
"If any of you lacks wisdom, let him ask of God, who gives to all liberally and without reproach, and it will be given to him." - James 1:5

3   **God Provides Peace**
"And the peace of God, which surpasses all understanding, will guard your hearts and minds through Christ Jesus." - Philippians 4:7

4   **God Gives Strength**
"He gives power to the weak, and to those who have no might He increases strength." - Isaiah 40:29

5   **God Heals**
"O Lord my God, I cried to You for help, and You healed me." - Psalm 30:2

FAITHVIBES

Deepening Your Prayer Life

10 Ways God Responds to Prayer

"Call to Me, and I will answer you, and show you great and mighty things, which you do not know".

JEREMIAH 33:3

6 **God Offers Guidance**
"I will instruct you and teach you in the way you should go; I will counsel you with my loving eye on you." - Psalm 32:8

7 **God Brings Comfort**
"Blessed are those who mourn, for they will be comforted." - Matthew 5:4

8 **God Delivers from Trouble**
"Call upon me in the day of trouble; I will deliver you, and you shall glorify me." - Psalm 50:15

9 **God Forgives Sins**
"If we confess our sins, He is faithful and just to forgive us our sins and to cleanse us from all unrighteousness." - 1 John 1:9

10 **God Opens Doors**
"Ask, and it will be given to you; seek, and you will find; knock, and it will be opened to you." - Matthew 7:7

FAITHVIBES
Deepening Your Prayer Life

DAY

1

Finding a Prayer Space

"But when you pray, go into your room,
close the door and pray to your Father,
who is unseen."

MATTHEW 6:6

Finding a quiet space to pray can make a world of difference in your spiritual life. Jesus emphasized the importance of withdrawing from distractions to communicate with God. Just as we set aside special moments for our loved ones, we must also carve out dedicated time and space for our relationship with God. Today, think about where you can create a personal sanctuary for prayer — whether it's a corner in your room, a spot in the garden, or even a quiet space during your commute. Remember, it's not about the location itself but the intentional act of setting apart time for God.

FAITHVIBES

Deepening Your Prayer Life

REFLECTION

*How can I create a quiet space for prayer
in my daily routine?*

_____

_____

_____

_____

_____

_____

_____

_____

_____

PRAYER

*Heavenly Father, guide me as I seek a quiet space to
meet with You daily. Help me create a place where I can
feel Your presence, free from distractions. May this
space become a sanctuary where my spirit is renewed
and my heart is filled with Your peace. Amen.*

FAITHVIBES

Deepening Your Prayer Life

JOURNAL YOUR THOUGHTS HERE

_____

_____

_____

_____

_____

_____

_____

_____

_____

_____

_____

_____

_____

_____

_____

_____

_____

_____

_____

_____

_____

FAITHVIBES

Deepening Your Prayer Life

DAY

2

Unceasing Prayer

"Pray without ceasing."

1 THESSALONIANS 5:17

"Pray without ceasing" may seem like an impossible task, but it is an invitation to keep God in our thoughts throughout the day. This doesn't mean we need to be on our knees every moment; rather, it's about maintaining a constant connection with God. A prayerful life is one where our hearts are in tune with His presence, whether we are working, driving, or even cooking dinner. Let today's focus be on inviting God into every aspect of your day, speaking with Him as a close friend, and listening to His gentle whispers.

FAITHVIBES
Deepening Your Prayer Life

REFLECTION

What does it mean to "pray without ceasing" in my own life?

_____

_____

_____

_____

_____

_____

_____

_____

PRAYER

God, teach me to keep my heart connected to You in every moment today. Amen.

FAITHVIBES

Deepening Your Prayer Life

JOURNAL YOUR THOUGHTS HERE

_____

_____

_____

_____

_____

_____

_____

_____

_____

_____

_____

_____

_____

_____

_____

_____

_____

_____

_____

FAITHVIBES

Deepening Your Prayer Life

Casting Your Cares

"Do not be anxious about anything, but in every situation, by prayer and petition, with thanksgiving, present your requests to God."

PHILIPPIANS 4:6

God invites us to bring all our worries and burdens to Him in prayer. Too often, we try to solve our problems on our own, forgetting that God is ready and willing to help. Today's scripture reminds us that in every situation, no matter how big or small, we should turn to God first. By presenting our requests to Him with a thankful heart, we acknowledge His sovereignty and trust in His provision. Let go of your anxieties today, and let God's peace fill your heart.

FAITHVIBES

Deepening Your Prayer Life

REFLECTION

What anxieties can I bring to God in prayer today?

PRAYER

Father, I surrender my worries to You and trust in Your peace. Amen.

FAITHVIBES

Deepening Your Prayer Life

JOURNAL YOUR THOUGHTS HERE

_____
_____
_____
_____
_____
_____
_____
_____
_____
_____
_____
_____
_____
_____
_____
_____
_____
_____
_____
_____

FAITHVIBES

Deepening Your Prayer Life

DAY

4

Praying for Others

"Therefore confess your sins to
each other and pray for each
other so that you may be healed.
The prayer of a righteous person
is powerful and effective."

JAMES 5:16

Praying for others is a powerful way to express love and compassion. When we intercede on behalf of others, we align our hearts with God's desire to bless and heal. James 5:16 reminds us that our prayers can be a source of healing and strength for others. Who in your life could use a prayer today? They could be enduring a health challenge, starting a new business or one of so many other scenarios. Take a moment to lift them up before God, believing that your prayers can make a real difference.

FAITHVIBES

Deepening Your Prayer Life

REFLECTION

Who do I know that would most benefit from a prayer of faith and sincerity today?

_____

_____

_____

_____

_____

_____

_____

_____

PRAYER

Lord, guide my heart to pray earnestly for those who need Your healing and grace. Amen.

FAITHVIBES

Deepening Your Prayer Life

JOURNAL YOUR THOUGHTS HERE

_____

_____

_____

_____

_____

_____

_____

_____

_____

_____

_____

_____

_____

_____

_____

_____

_____

_____

_____

FAITHVIBES
Deepening Your Prayer Life

Drawing Near to God

"The Lord is near to all who call on him, to all who call on him in truth."

PSALM 145:18

God promises to draw near to us when we call on Him with a sincere heart. Prayer is not just about asking for things; it's about seeking a deeper relationship with our Creator. When we approach God with honesty and openness, we invite His presence into our lives. Today, focus on coming to God with a heart full of truth and transparency. Share your hopes, fears, and dreams with Him, knowing that He is close and attentive to your every word.

Remember to always be open to hear God speak to you as a response to your prayer.

FAITHVIBES

Deepening Your Prayer Life

REFLECTION

*How can I draw nearer to
God in my prayers?*

_____

_____

_____

_____

_____

_____

_____

_____

PRAYER

*God, draw near to me as I seek You
with a sincere and open heart. Amen.*

FAITHVIBES

Deepening Your Prayer Life

JOURNAL YOUR THOUGHTS HERE

_____

_____

_____

_____

_____

_____

_____

_____

_____

_____

_____

_____

_____

_____

_____

_____

_____

_____

_____

_____

FAITHVIBES

Deepening Your Prayer Life

The Spirit's Help

*"In the same way, the Spirit helps us
in our weakness. We do not know
what we ought to pray for, but the
Spirit himself intercedes for us
through wordless groans."*

ROMANS 8:26

Sometimes, we struggle to find the right words to pray or feel overwhelmed by our situations. But we are not alone; the Holy Spirit is our Helper. He intercedes for us, even when we don't know what to say. Trust that the Spirit knows your heart and is already lifting your needs to God. When you feel weak or unsure, lean on the Spirit's strength and let Him guide your prayers.

FAITHVIBES
Deepening Your Prayer Life

REFLECTION

When have I felt the Holy Spirit
interceding for me in prayer?

_____

_____

_____

_____

_____

_____

_____

_____

PRAYER

Holy Spirit, intercede for me in my
weakness and guide my prayers today.
Amen.

FAITHVIBES

Deepening Your Prayer Life

JOURNAL YOUR THOUGHTS HERE

_____

_____

_____

_____

_____

_____

_____

_____

_____

_____

_____

_____

_____

_____

_____

_____

_____

_____

FAITHVIBES

Deepening Your Prayer Life

DAY

7

Believing in Prayer

*"Therefore I tell you, whatever
you ask for in prayer, believe
that you have received it, and it
will be yours."*

MARK 11:24

Prayer without faith is like a bird without wings —
it cannot soar. Jesus teaches us to pray with belief,
trusting that God is both willing, able and excited
to answer. Taking this further, there are certain
things that are our rights as believers. For
example, Paul said God would supply all of his
need. If we look at it He was confident that
provision was his right as a believer. He expects
God's provision. Today, bring your requests before
God with a heart full of faith. Remember, it's not
about the size of your faith because a mustard seed
can of faith can move mountains, but
understanding greatness of the One in whom you
place your faith.

FAITHVIBES

Deepening Your Prayer Life

REFLECTION

What prayer requests do I need to believe God will answer?

_____

_____

_____

_____

_____

_____

_____

_____

_____

PRAYER

Lord, strengthen my faith to believe in the power of my prayers and Your promises. Amen.

FAITHVIBES

Deepening Your Prayer Life

JOURNAL YOUR THOUGHTS HERE

_____

_____

_____

_____

_____

_____

_____

_____

_____

_____

_____

_____

_____

_____

_____

_____

_____

_____

_____

_____

_____

Vigilance in Prayer

"And pray in the Spirit on all occasions with all kinds of prayers and requests. With this in mind, be alert and always keep on praying for all the Lord's people."

EPHESIANS 6:18

Being vigilant in prayer means being watchful and alert, not just for our needs but for the needs of others. Prayer is an ongoing conversation with God that doesn't end when we say, "Amen." Today, make it a priority to stay alert to the Spirit's prompting, praying for your family, friends, and even strangers. Your prayers can make a difference in someone's life.

FAITHVIBES
Deepening Your Prayer Life

REFLECTION

How can I be more vigilant in my prayers for others?

_____

_____

_____

_____

_____

_____

_____

_____

PRAYER

*God, help me remain alert and
persistent in my prayers, lifting up all
who need Your grace. Amen.*

FAITHVIBES

Deepening Your Prayer Life

JOURNAL YOUR THOUGHTS HERE

_____

_____

_____

_____

_____

_____

_____

_____

_____

_____

_____

_____

_____

_____

_____

_____

_____

God's Promise to Hear

"The righteous cry out, and the Lord hears them; he delivers them from all their troubles."

PSALM 34:17

It is comforting to know that God hears us when we cry out to Him. He is not distant or indifferent but is always attentive to the cries of His children. Even in times of trouble, we can have confidence that God is listening and ready to deliver us. Today, hold on to this promise and approach God with boldness, knowing He is awaiting your approach and is ready to exchange your answer or solution. The key here is knowing that not only does God hear you, but prayer is a conversation and in prayer He speaks in return.

FAITHVIBES

Deepening Your Prayer Life

REFLECTION

How does God's promise to hear the righteous comfort me today?

_____

_____

_____

_____

_____

_____

_____

_____

_____

PRAYER

Lord, thank You for hearing me and delivering me from any trouble I face. Amen.

FAITHVIBES
Deepening Your Prayer Life

JOURNAL YOUR THOUGHTS HERE

_____
_____
_____
_____
_____
_____
_____
_____
_____
_____
_____
_____
_____
_____
_____
_____
_____

FAITHVIBES

Deepening Your Prayer Life

Fervent Prayer

*"The prayer of a righteous person
is powerful and effective."*

JAMES 5:16 (NIV)

Fervent prayer is marked by intensity, passion, and persistence. It's more than a casual conversation; it's a heartfelt plea to God, rooted in faith and knowledge of the Word of God. James reminds us that such prayers are powerful and effective. Today, pray fervently for what matters most to you, trusting in God's word and His ability to move mightily on your behalf.

FAITHVIBES
Deepening Your Prayer Life

REFLECTION

*What does fervent prayer mean to me,
and how can I practice it more earnestly?*

_____

_____

_____

_____

_____

_____

_____

_____

PRAYER

*Lord, help me pray with passion,
faith, and urgency, knowing You hear
and answer. Amen.*

FAITHVIBES

Deepening Your Prayer Life

JOURNAL YOUR THOUGHTS HERE

FAITHVIBES
Deepening Your Prayer Life

Persistence in Prayer

"So I say to you, ask and keep on asking and it shall be given you; seek and keep on seeking and you shall find; knock and keep on knocking and the door shall be opened to you"

LUKE 11:9

Jesus teaches us the importance of persistence in prayer, reminding us not to lose heart when answers aren't immediate. God values our perseverance and faithfulness, often using the waiting period to deepen our trust in Him. Some opportunities only appear when we actively ask or seek them out, and certain doors require the right "access code" to open. Jesus assures us that doors will open when we ask. So today, continue to ask, seek, and knock with confidence, trusting that God hears every prayer and will respond in His perfect timing.

FAITHVIBES

Deepening Your Prayer Life

REFLECTION

What prayers have I given up on that I need to persist in asking for?

_____

_____

_____

_____

_____

_____

_____

_____

PRAYER

God, give me the strength and patience to persist in prayer, trusting in Your perfect timing. Amen.

FAITHVIBES

Deepening Your Prayer Life

JOURNAL YOUR THOUGHTS HERE

_____

_____

_____

_____

_____

_____

_____

_____

_____

_____

_____

_____

_____

_____

_____

_____

_____

_____

_____

_____

_____

DAY

12

Morning Prayers

"In the morning, Lord, you hear my voice; in the morning I lay my requests before you and wait expectantly."

PSALM 5:3

Starting the day with prayer sets the tone for the entire day. Morning prayer can prepare you for or even remove things that would try to negatively impact your day. Conversely, morning prayer can also invite great opportunities into your day. Morning prayers are an act of placing God first, seeking His guidance, protection, strategy, and blessings before facing the challenges of the day. Make it a habit to spend the first moments of your day with God, thanking Him for an amazing day filled with the expectation of His plans fulfilled in your life.

FAITHVIBES

Deepening Your Prayer Life

REFLECTION

*How can I make morning prayers a
regular part of my routine?*

PRAYER

*Father, help me begin each day with
You, bringing my needs and desires
before You. Amen.*

FAITHVIBES

Deepening Your Prayer Life

JOURNAL YOUR THOUGHTS HERE

FAITHVIBES

Deepening Your Prayer Life

DAY

13

Approaching God with Confidence

"Let us then approach God's throne of grace with confidence, so that we may receive mercy and find grace to help us in our time of need."

HEBREWS 4:16

God invites us to approach His throne with boldness, free from fear or hesitation, and filled with confidence. As our loving Father, He welcomes us warmly, encouraging us to come to Him in prayer with the expectation of His response. As John 1:15 reminds us, if we know that He listens to us in whatever we ask, we can also be assured that our requests are granted as our present possessions. Today, accept this invitation and approach God with the assurance that He is eager to listen and provide.

FAITHVIBES

Deepening Your Prayer Life

REFLECTION

How can I approach God's throne of grace with more confidence today? What areas of my life am I hesitant or fearful of bringing before God?

_____

_____

_____

_____

_____

_____

_____

_____

PRAYER

Lord, give me confidence to come before You, knowing You are ready to provide grace and mercy. Amen.

FAITHVIBES

Deepening Your Prayer Life

JOURNAL YOUR THOUGHTS HERE

_____

_____

_____

_____

_____

_____

_____

_____

_____

_____

_____

_____

_____

_____

_____

_____

_____

_____

_____

FAITHVIBES
Deepening Your Prayer Life

DAY
14

Thankfulness in Prayer

"Devote yourselves to prayer,
being watchful and thankful."
COLOSSIANS 4:2

A heart filled with gratitude transforms our prayers and strengthens our relationship with God. By focusing on thankfulness, we recognize God's goodness in every situation, even during challenges. It demonstrates our trust in His promises and faithfulness. It's easy to get caught up in what isn't happening for us, but we must remember to give thanks for all that is happening. Today, take a moment to thank God for the blessings in your life and see how gratitude can shift your perspective and draw you closer to Him.

FAITHVIBES

Deepening Your Prayer Life

REFLECTION

How can I be more watchful and thankful in my prayers?
What is one thing that I can be thankful for in my prayers today?

_____

_____

_____

_____

_____

_____

_____

_____

PRAYER

God, help me to see Your goodness all
around me and to express my
gratitude in every prayer. Amen.

FAITHVIBES

Deepening Your Prayer Life

JOURNAL YOUR THOUGHTS HERE

_____

_____

_____

_____

_____

_____

_____

_____

_____

_____

_____

_____

_____

_____

_____

_____

_____

_____

_____

_____

FAITHVIBES

Deepening Your Prayer Life

Answered Prayers

"I cried out to him with my mouth; his praise was on my tongue. If I had cherished sin in my heart, the Lord would not have listened; but God has surely listened and has heard my prayer."

PSALM 66:17-20

Reflect on the times God has answered your prayers, big or small, and let those moments strengthen your faith. Remember that God hears your prayers. Sometimes we focus on the answers that were in line with what we wanted, but God's response is always what He knows is best. Give thanks for His faithfulness and trust that He continues to listen and respond according to His perfect will.

FAITHVIBES

Deepening Your Prayer Life

REFLECTION

*When has God answered my prayers in a
way that strengthened my faith?*

_____

_____

_____

_____

_____

_____

_____

_____

PRAYER

*Lord, thank You for the ways You
have answered my prayers and
strengthened my faith. Amen.*

FAITHVIBES
Deepening Your Prayer Life

JOURNAL YOUR THOUGHTS HERE

_____
_____
_____
_____
_____
_____
_____
_____
_____
_____
_____
_____
_____
_____
_____
_____
_____
_____
_____

FAITHVIBES
Deepening Your Prayer Life

DAY
16

Faith in Prayer

"If you believe, you will receive whatever you ask for in prayer."
MATTHEW 21:22

Faith is a key component of prayer. As Matthew 17:20 reminds us, "if you have faith as small as a mustard seed, you can say to this mountain, 'Move from here to there,' and it will move; and nothing will be impossible for you." Today, focus on strengthening your belief that God hears and answers. Trust that your prayers, grounded in faith, have the power to move not only mountainous problems away from you, but can move good things to your here and now.

FAITHVIBES

Deepening Your Prayer Life

REFLECTION

*How can I strengthen my faith to believe
in the power of my prayers?*

_____

_____

_____

_____

_____

_____

_____

_____

PRAYER

*Lord, increase my faith so that I may
believe wholeheartedly in the power of
my prayers. Amen.*

FAITHVIBES

Deepening Your Prayer Life

JOURNAL YOUR THOUGHTS HERE

FAITHVIBES

Deepening Your Prayer Life

Pouring Out Your Heart

"Trust in him at all times, you people; pour out your hearts to him, for God is our refuge."

PSALM 62:8

"Trust in Him at all times, you people; pour out your hearts to Him, for God is our refuge. Selah." God extends an invitation for you to open your heart to Him and rely on Him as your safe haven. In moments of uncertainty, don't hold back your worries, fears, or dreams. Cast them all before God (1 Peter 5:7), assured that He listens and cares deeply for you. Embrace the comfort that comes from knowing you are never alone, and that His strength and love are always there to support you through life's challenges.

FAITHVIBES

Deepening Your Prayer Life

REFLECTION

What burdens do I need to pour out before God today?

_____

_____

_____

_____

_____

_____

_____

_____

PRAYER

Father, I pour out my heart to You today, trusting You to be my refuge and strength. Amen.

FAITHVIBES

Deepening Your Prayer Life

JOURNAL YOUR THOUGHTS HERE

FAITHVIBES

Deepening Your Prayer Life

DAY

18

Praise in Prayer

"About midnight Paul and Silas were praying and singing hymns to God, and the other prisoners were listening to them."

ACTS 16:25

Praise has the power to shift our spiritual outlook and change our circumstances, even in the darkest moments. For Paul and Silas, praise was a key that released a miracle. Their praise invited heaven to initiate a jailbreak, setting them completely free. Like Paul and Silas, choose to praise God today, no matter what challenges you face, trusting that He is in control. You will begin to see your praise break the chains and unlock spiritual and emotional prisons that thought they could hold you. Your praise is a powerful prayer tool!

54

FAITHVIBES

Deepening Your Prayer Life

REFLECTION

How can I incorporate praise into my prayers, even during difficult times?

_____

_____

_____

_____

_____

_____

_____

_____

PRAYER

God, teach me to praise You in all circumstances, knowing that You are always in control. Amen.

FAITHVIBES

Deepening Your Prayer Life

JOURNAL YOUR THOUGHTS HERE

_____

_____

_____

_____

_____

_____

_____

_____

_____

_____

_____

_____

_____

_____

_____

_____

_____

_____

_____

_____

_____

DAY

19

Aligning with God's Will

*"If you remain in me and my
words remain in you, ask
whatever you wish, and it will be
done for you."*

JOHN 15:7

When our desires align with God's will, our prayers become powerful. God created you as a free moral agent, meaning you can in essence do what you want to. When we align our lives with God's will you are sacrificing your will for His. God receives this as an act of worship and honor. Reflect today on whether your prayers are in line with God's word and His plans for your life, and seek to align your heart with His.

FAITHVIBES

Deepening Your Prayer Life

5 Ways To Discover God's Will

Seek God's Guidance Through Prayer

"If any of you lacks wisdom, let him ask of God, who gives to all liberally and without reproach, and it will be given to him." - James 1:5

Praying for wisdom is essential when seeking God's will. God promises to provide clarity and understanding to those who ask sincerely.

Study God's Word Regularly

"Your word is a lamp to my feet and a light to my path." - Psalm 119:105

Scripture is a primary way God reveals His will. Studying the Bible helps us align our desires with His commands and principles.

Pay Attention to the Holy Spirit's Prompting

"But when he, the Spirit of truth, comes, he will guide you into all the truth." - John 16:13

The Holy Spirit guides believers into truth. Being sensitive to the Spirit's promptings helps us discern God's will in various situations.
Seek Godly Counsel

FAITHVIBES

Deepening Your Prayer Life

Seek Godly Counsel

"Where there is no guidance, a people falls, but in an abundance of counselors there is safety." - Proverbs 11:14

Seeking advice from mature, godly individuals provides insight and confirmation when discerning God's direction for our lives.

Look for Confirmation Through Circumstances

"And we know that in all things God works for the good of those who love him, who have been called according to his purpose." - Romans 8:28

God often uses circumstances to confirm His will. Observing how events unfold can help us understand His plan and timing.

FAITHVIBES

Deepening Your Prayer Life

REFLECTION

*How can I align my desires with God's
will to see more answered prayers?*

_____

_____

_____

_____

_____

_____

_____

_____

PRAYER

*Lord, align my heart with Yours so
that my prayers reflect Your will and
Your goodness. Amen.*

FAITHVIBES

Deepening Your Prayer Life

JOURNAL YOUR THOUGHTS HERE

_____

_____

_____

_____

_____

_____

_____

_____

_____

_____

_____

_____

_____

_____

_____

_____

_____

_____

_____

_____

FAITHVIBES

Deepening Your Prayer Life

DAY

20

Praying with Empathy

*"He will respond to the prayer of
the destitute; he will not despise
their plea."*

PSALM 102:17

Praying with empathy is a powerful way to connect our hearts with the struggles and pain of others. It allows us to step into their shoes, feel their burdens, and lift them up before God with genuine compassion. When we pray with empathy, we become intercessors, standing in the gap for those who may be too weary, overwhelmed, or broken to pray for themselves. Today, take a moment to think of someone who is going through a difficult time, whether it's a friend, a loved one, or even a stranger, and pray declaring God's word of healing and restoration over their lives.

FAITHVIBES

Deepening Your Prayer Life

REFLECTION

*How can I pray with empathy for those
who are hurting or in need?*

_____

_____

_____

_____

_____

_____

_____

_____

_____

PRAYER

*God, help me to feel the pain of
others and to pray with sincere
compassion for them. Amen.*

FAITHVIBES

Deepening Your Prayer Life

JOURNAL YOUR THOUGHTS HERE

FAITH VIBES
Deepening Your Prayer Life

DAY
21

Reflecting on Prayer Growth

"May these words of my mouth
and this meditation of my heart
be pleasing in your sight, Lord,
my Rock and my Redeemer."

Look back on the past three weeks and reflect on how your prayer life has changed. Celebrate the growth and identify areas where you can continue to develop and deepen your relationship with God.

FAITHVIBES

Deepening Your Prayer Life

REFLECTION

How has my prayer life grown over the past three weeks, and what do I want to improve next?

_____

_____

_____

_____

_____

_____

_____

_____

_____

PRAYER

Lord, thank You for growing me through this journey. Help me to continue deepening my prayer life. Amen.

FAITHVIBES

Deepening Your Prayer Life

JOURNAL YOUR THOUGHTS HERE

---

www.ingramcontent.com/pod-product-compliance
Lightning Source LLC
LaVergne TN
LVHW061221060426
835508LV00014B/1390